Protect Our Planet

Polluted Air

Angela Royston

www.heinemannlibrary.co.uk
Visit our website to find out more information about Heinemann Library books.

To order:
☎ Phone +44 (0) 1865 888066
🗎 Fax +44 (0) 1865 314091
💻 Visit www.heinemannlibrary.co.uk

Heinemann Library is an imprint of Capstone Global Library Limited, a company incorporated in England and Wales having its registered office at 7 Pilgrim Street, London, EC4V 6LB – Registered company number: 6695582

Heinemann is a registered trademark of Pearson Education Limited, under licence to Capstone Global Library Limited

Editorial: Sian Smith and Cassie Mayer
Design: Joanna Hinton-Malivoire
Picture research: Melissa Allison, Fiona Orbell and Erica Martin
Production: Duncan Gilbert

Printed and bound in China by South China Printing Co. Ltd.

ISBN 978 0 431 08475 6 (hardback)
12 11 10 09 08
10 9 8 7 6 5 4 3 2 1

ISBN 978 0 431 08481 7 (paperback)
13 12 11 10 09
10 9 8 7 6 5 4 3 2 1

British Library Cataloguing in Publication Data
Royston, Angela
   Polluted air. - (Protect our planet)
   1. Air - Pollution - Juvenile literature 2. Air quality management - Juvenile literature
   I. Title
   363.7'392

Acknowledgements
The publishers would like to thank the following for permission to reproduce photographs: © Alamy pp.**16** (David Robertson, **11** (moodboard), **23** (Paul Glendell), **20** (Philip Bigg), **12** (Tom Uhlman); © Corbis pp.**22**, **25** (Abode, Beateworks), **27** (Andrew Fox), **7** (moodboard), **24** (Paulo Fridman), **26** (Roger Ressmeyer); © Ecoscene pp.**17** (Erik Schaffer), **6** (Fritz Polking); © Getty Images p.**13** (Photodisc); © Panos pp.**15** (Dermot Tatlow), **29** (Mark Henley), **10** (Simon Horton); © Pearson Education Ltd p.**19** (David Rigg); © Photolibrary pp.**14**(Japack Photo Library), **5** (Nordicphotos), **28** (Rob Cousins), **21** (Schmuel Thaler); © Science Photo Library p.**4** (Tom Van Sant, Geosphere Project, Santa Monica); © Still Pictures p.**8** (F.Herrmann)

Cover photograph of traffic in winter reproduced with permission of © Masterfile (Gary Gerovac).

Every effort has been made to contact copyright holders of any material reproduced in this book. Any omissions will be rectified in subsequent printings if notice is given to the publishers.

Contents

Any words appearing in the text in bold, **like this**, are explained in the Glossary.

What is air?

Air is a mixture of gases that surround our planet, the Earth. You cannot see the air, but you can feel it when you run and when you fly a kite.

The thin band of air around the Earth is shown in bright blue.

Clouds are made of tiny drops of water in the air. The air stretches for several miles above the clouds. The air becomes thinner the higher it is above the ground.

Why is air important?

Oxygen is one of the gases in air. Living things need oxygen to stay alive. Animals breathe in oxygen to get the energy they need to move around.

The faster an animal runs, the more oxygen it needs to breathe in.

Carbon dioxide is another gas that is in the air. Humans and other animals breathe out carbon dioxide.

Where does oxygen come from?

Plants make **oxygen** when they create plant food. Their leaves take in **carbon dioxide** from the air. They use sunlight to change carbon dioxide and water into plant food.

Plants make their own food.

When plants make plant food, they also make oxygen. The oxygen escapes into the air. This gives more oxygen for animals to breathe in.

Plants use water, sunlight, and carbon dioxide from the air to make plant food.

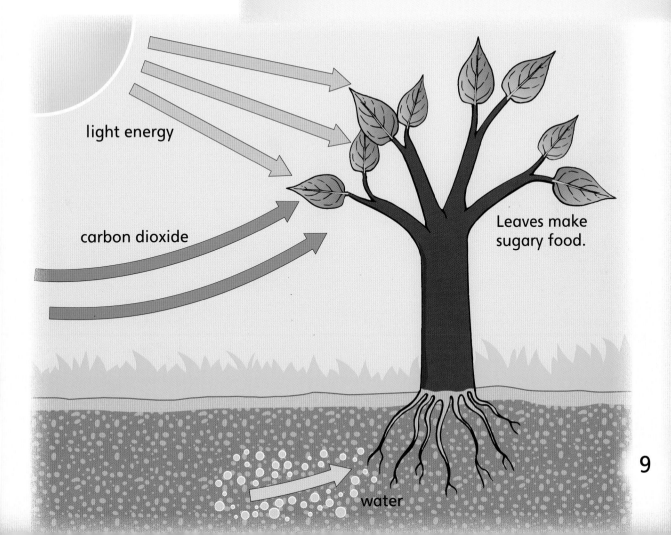

light energy

carbon dioxide

Leaves make sugary food.

water

What is air pollution?

Dirt or other harmful things in the air are called air **pollution**. The air in cities is usually more **polluted** than in the countryside. Most pollution is caused by vehicles, factories, and **power stations**.

Some big cities have a layer of pollution hanging over them.

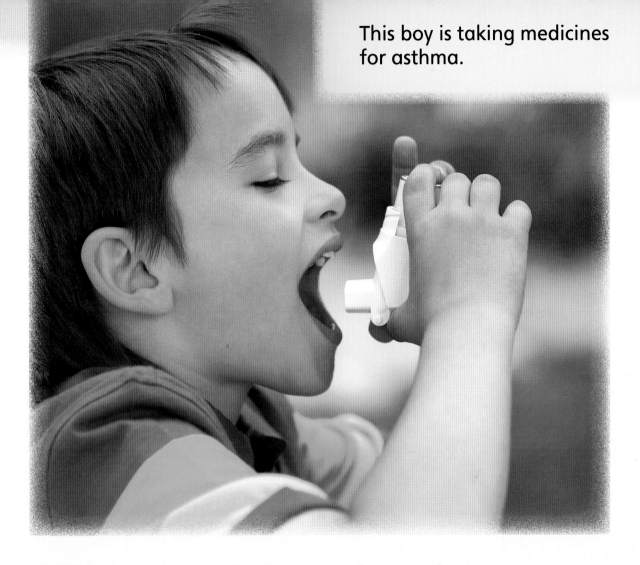

This boy is taking medicines for asthma.

If the air is very dirty, people can become ill. They may also have trouble breathing. **Asthma** is an illness that makes it difficult to breathe. People with asthma may have an asthma attack when the air is very polluted.

How do vehicles pollute the air?

Aeroplanes, cars, trucks, and other vehicles have engines that burn **fuel** to make them work. Almost all fuel is made from **oil**. As vehicles burn fuel, they create **waste** gases.

Cars release waste gases into the air.

The waste gases escape into the air. The gases mix with the air and **pollute** it. Waste gases include **carbon dioxide** and several poisonous gases.

13

What else causes air pollution?

Most factories and **power stations** cause air **pollution**. Factories make many kinds of things. For example, toys, clothes, cars, and even some foods are made in factories. Many factories create **waste chemicals** that **pollute** the air.

The air pollution shown here comes from a factory.

The coal used by power stations has to be brought up from under the ground.

Power stations make **electricity**. We use electricity to light our rooms and to run televisions, computers, and other machines. Most power stations burn **fuels** such as coal or **oil** to make electricity. Burning coal and oil makes waste gases that pollute the air.

Polluted rain

Rain is drops of water that form in thick clouds. **Waste** gases from factories and **power stations** mix with the drops of water. The gases **pollute** the rain. Sometimes rain also contains **soot** and other bits of dirt.

Half of this building has been cleaned. The other half is still black from soot and dirt in the rain.

Acid rain has eaten away some of the carving on this wall.

Polluted rain is called **acid rain**. Acid rain damages buildings. It can also kill trees. When acid rain flows into lakes, it can kill fish and other animals.

The ozone layer

The **ozone layer** is a layer of ozone gas that is high above the clouds. The ozone layer protects us from the harmful rays of the Sun.

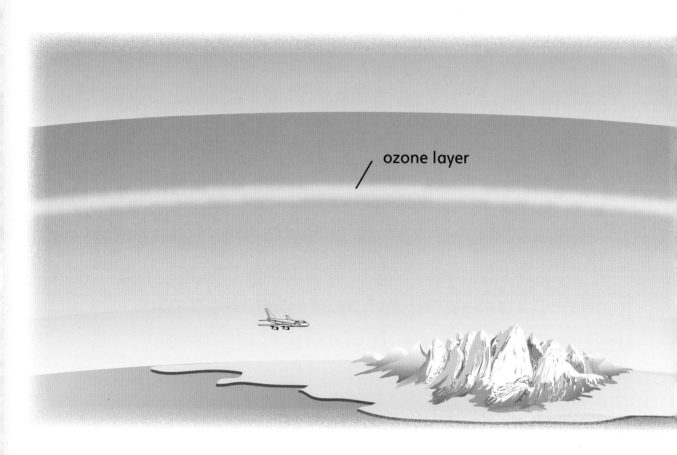

ozone layer

Some of the **chemicals** that are used to make refrigerators work can damage the ozone layer.

Some kinds of air **pollution** destroy some of the ozone in the ozone layer. When ozone is destroyed the ozone layer becomes thinner. Then it does not protect us as well from the Sun.

Cleaner cars

Scientists are finding new ways of reducing air **pollution**. They are making cars and other vehicles that make less pollution. Some vehicles run on **natural gas**. Natural gas makes less pollution than petrol.

This special taxi runs on natural gas.

These cars use electric motors.

Other vehicles use an **electric motor** instead of an engine that burns petrol. **Hybrid** cars use an electric motor and a small petrol engine. They create less pollution than regular cars.

Clean ways of making electricity

New kinds of **power stations** are being built. They use sunlight, the wind, or running water to make **electricity**. These power stations make no **pollution**.

These panels use sunlight to make electricity. They do not make **carbon dioxide**.

wind turbine

People can make their own electricity without making pollution. A small **wind turbine** on the roof of a building can make enough electricity to run the lights and computers inside.

Cleaner factories

Some factories are becoming cleaner. These factories make less air **pollution** by trapping the dirt and **waste** gases before they reach the air.

This factory makes a small amount of air pollution.

The hood over this cooker has a filter that cleans the air.

Factories trap dirt by **filtering** the waste gases. A filter works like a coffee filter. It traps things that are too big to pass through it.

Getting rid of rubbish

People who live in rich countries create a lot of rubbish. When rubbish is burned, it **pollutes** the air. Some of the gases are poisonous.

All the rubbish here is being taken to be burned.

Plastic, paper, metal, and glass can all be collected for recycling.

One way to cut air **pollution** is to make less rubbish. You can help to do this by buying things that do not have much packaging. You can also help by **recycling** as much rubbish as possible.

Avoiding air pollution

There are several things you can do to avoid breathing in air **pollution**. When you walk or cycle, try to avoid busy roads. If possible, keep to quiet roads and back streets.

In some places special paths are made for cyclists to use. These help them to keep away from busy roads.

In very **polluted** places, people wear face masks so that they do not breathe in polluted air.

Some countries are working to limit the amount of pollution they create. They set limits for how much pollution factories and **power stations** can create. The more people work together to reduce air pollution, the cleaner our air will be.

Glossary

acid rain rain that kills leaves and eats away at buildings

asthma illness that can make it difficult to breathe

carbon dioxide one of the gases in the air

chemical substance that things are made of

electricity form of energy used to make machines work

electric motor engine that uses electricity to make something work

filtering using a fine mesh to separate solids, such as dust, from a liquid or gas

fuel substance such as gas, wood, or coal that is burned to give heat, light, or power

hybrid mixture of two or more things

natural gas gas that burns easily and is used for fuel

oil liquid that burns easily and is used for fuel

oxygen one of the gases in the air

ozone layer layer of ozone gas that protects us from the Sun's rays

pollute make dirty

pollution dirt or waste gases or chemicals

power station building where electricity is made

recycling processing used materials so that they can be used again

soot black dust made when coal and other things are burned

waste things that are thrown out because they are not wanted any more

wind turbine machine that makes electricity using blades that spin in the wind

Find out more

Books to read

I can help: I can help clean our air, Viv Smith
(Franklin Watts Ltd, 2001)

Reduce, Reuse, Recycle: Plastic, Alexandra Fix
(Heinemann Library, 2007)

Websites to visit

www.epa.gov/kids/air.htm
This website tells you about air pollution and what you can do to help keep the air clean.

Index